chasing shadows
living with P.T.S.D.

For more information, email : chasingshadowsbook@gmail.com

©

#EdnaDaRocha

#chasingshadows

ISBN 978-0-7961-7841-1

Dedication

To my knight, my husband, Rocky
And our Angel daughters, Tania and Shante
30th November 2015

.

Medical Acronyms Used in This Book:

P.T.S.D. - Post Traumatic Stress Disorder
   A disorder characterized by failure to recover after experiencing or witnessing a terrifying
   event.
   The condition may last months or years, with triggers that can bring back
   memories of the trauma accompanied by intense emotional and physical reactions.
   O.C.D. - Obsessive Compulsive Disorder
   (OCD) features a pattern of unwanted thoughts and fears (obsessions) that lead to repetitive
   behaviours (compulsions) interfering with daily activities and causing significant stress.
   E.M.T. - Emergency Medical Technician
   Emergency Medical Technicians are educated in assessing a patient and determining if any
   life threatening injuries or illnesses may be present.

Introduction

It should be noted that this book was not written with malicious intent toward anyone mentioned in its pages. It is solely a recollection of my thoughts and emotions as I journey through Post Traumatic Stress Disorder.

The thoughts and processes expressed in this narrative are solely those I experienced as events took place and emotions flowed from day to day.

It not only includes what happened and was and still is experienced by women but also the experiences of men and children who may have gone through something similar in their lives.

This book is for all of you. Know that you are not the only one and that exceptional help is available. You just have to take the first step and find it.

Foreword

I always thought and verbalized;
"I would do anything to protect my daughters and my husband.
I just didn't think it would be this."

Edna da Rocha

One

Try dying every day
To your old self...
So that you emerge
Renewed and young again
As the tired mind
Sheds its load...

KRISTIN ZAMBUCKA

Two

I am no hero. I'm just a mother and a wife who tried to save her family.

I still wake most nights reliving the incident that has so changed our lives.

Whether it's trying to fall asleep as I mull each step, or waking up in fear, I still battle this demon inside.

Our lives, as a family and as individuals, have changed forever, mine especially. There is no going back. There is only forward, and forward seems daunting.

Our normal no longer exists, and together we must find our way to a new "normal."

Yet I no longer understand how to measure any kind of normal.

To become the person I am today, I first became the very devil I despised. As I look back, I hated the person I was forced to become. I hated what I did and its aftermath.

Three

The pain is not necessarily physical or even visual — perhaps because it is not visible, someone suffering with Post Traumatic Stress Disorder is often misunderstood.

I'm still living with it.

It's been a long arduous journey. Every day I'm still careful and apprehensive as I put one foot in front of the other.

I never thought I would find myself in this place. It's so overwhelming that I'm still trying to understand it, trying to record my experiences, feelings, and thoughts is emotionally and mentally draining. As I type each word with care and consideration, tears fill my eyes and run down my cheeks.

Not everything pours out at once. Rather, it's a fountain of emotions that I'm constantly, unwittingly holding in check.

I'm ashamed to admit that at times I wonder if my family would have been better off had I not survived this ordeal.

Four

We all have times when life feels hard
when we feel frustrated and just want
to hide away. If that's you right now,
don't worry – every caterpillar has to rest
to become a butterfly, and soon you'll find
your wings again. In the mean-time,
let your Angels wrap you in theirs.
You are so loved.
_____ Anna Taylor _____
(Kelly's Treehouse)

As I live each day,
May I make a difference
And touch one heart...
Each day, it is my goal
To bring smiles and laughter
Into a soul!
_____ Author Unknown _____

Five – Backstory

I'm usually pedantic and rather particular, but sometimes, jokingly or not, I've been labelled an Obsessive Compulsive, a person who suffers from OCD.

I've always seen myself as an ardent, involved wife, and parent who pays close attention to conversations and the needs of her family.

Now, however, I'm finding it difficult to recall a conversation of an hour ago. The best way I can describe it is that, to me, it's as though the conversation never took place. I'm unable to digest information at a normal pace. My memory is slow and muddled most of the time, and frequently, my concentration seems to lapse. To others, I appear cold and distant, though my mind is trying to process the information communicated and my responses are at times measured and gradual.

Early in this journey, I became disappointed with myself for not recalling conversations or events. I only knew NOW. Not five minutes ago, not what I needed to do later or tomorrow. That no longer existed in my world.

As time passed, I realized that my mental health had taken a toll on my loved ones. Yet I can't remember any point when they made me feel so.

During sessions with my psychiatrist and psychologist, I understood that while suppressing memories of the traumatic event, I'd also suppressed good memories. For several years, that forgetfulness has been part of everyday existence. I cannot remember the person I was, let alone contend with my new "normal".

By nature, I'm not much of a talker, but over time I got frustrated when I found it difficult to have a conversation because I couldn't remember words or how to construct a sentence. What was once a simple conversation became a daunting task.

I became oblivious to things I may have said or done, every date, every event — even putting together the words to write this book.

At times, I couldn't remember where I had put my notes for my manuscript.

I became impatient with myself and resentful as I could not recall any of my good memories. They just didn't and still don't exist. I saw my memory as an assortment of locked drawers, for few of which I had the key.

My conversations were limited to a few words. When I did remember words, it became another struggle to verbalize them without stumbling.

Six – Trying to Deal with the Hand I was Dealt

For the first year, I tried to deal with the "unknown" on my own, not really knowing what was happening. I went about my day pretending all was okay. I had to be strong, so I could keep my family going daily, but inside, I was crumbling. It wasn't an instant feeling of a rock falling, but rather a steady degradation.

Getting up every morning, I thought, "*this is the one, it has to be better*." But each day I was knocked down by the reality of what had happened. I didn't and still don't comprehend what I'm going through.

The incident plays over and over in my mind. The flashbacks are endless, leaving me in a constant state of anxiety. All my senses are on hyper-alert every second of every day.

I couldn't make peace with the raw feeling of struggling to survive, and I'm still struggling with the brutal truth, trying to take one day at a time.

The intensity of the emotions triggered by P.T.S.D. will make any reasonable person question their sanity. I'd always been the strong one in the family, the "pillar." Now I was completely broken.

Looking back, I realize that I was trying to grasp something, that even my faith couldn't still my heart. Even today, I'm not sure what I was grasping for. Survival? Sanity?

A year after the trauma, I realized that something was severely wrong with me, and it was recommended that I see both a psychologist and a psychiatrist.

Seven – The Reasons Behind It All

Our home, usually a place of quiet and serenity, was replaced with the cacophony of police coming and going.

I had removed myself from the scene of madness to sit in a quiet space on the stairs, trying to comprehend what had just transpired.

I'm always surprised when people use the word "surreal." But that day, "surreal" was the only word to describe what was unfolding before my eyes and what had occurred just a few hours before.

After some time had passed on that fateful day, I was called back to our bedroom. My eye caught the motionless body still lying on the floor. It was covered, but a slow trickle of blood was escaping beneath it. To my left, I saw my husband, whom the police had asked to strip to his underwear so that photographs could be taken of his bruised body and bleeding knees. Granted, this was to collect evidence. Just a few hours earlier, our sanctuary had been invaded. Now we were back in our bedroom with more strangers. Like a flash flood, dizziness and nausea overcame me. I had to leave the room in a hurry, randomly bumping into police officers on my way down the stairs. My mind wanted to explode. It was all too much to absorb.

Police officers were coming and going, some hovering, some asking if I was all right, others shaking my hand and congratulating me on my bravery. I stared blankly into unknown faces without comprehending the mayhem around me. I was uncertain and on edge. I feared being arrested and taken from my home in handcuffs.

Since the early hours of the morning, our kind neighbour, had been popping in to comfort me, hugging me and holding my hand whilst telling me that social media had lit up with our incident. Someone had shared the information on a social platform. I stared at her blankly and politely thanked her for her kindness, not really understanding what she had just shared with me. To be honest, I've never been much of a social media person.

At some point, an Emergency Medical Technician arrived and suggested giving me an injection of something or other to keep me calm while people surged into our once-quiet home. I declined. I thought my usual coffee and cigarettes would do the trick. I thought I was still in control.

I'm a naturally strong woman who often referred to herself as a "tough cookie." I could keep calm during the storm, always there for those in need. That day, it seemed the tables had turned.

Our domestic, arrived for the week, confused and in shock from what she saw. Unfortunately, she was not allowed into the house, but her concern over us never wavered. I wanted to hug her and explain that we were all safe, but I was asked to avoid going outside at all costs. My husband took it upon himself to explain the situation to her, and I'm sure the police did, too.

Sometime later, friends arrived to comfort us and to be sure we were coping. They kindly offered to bring their live-in domestic to help clean up the scene after the police had completed their investigation. I don't recall answering them, but I am sure that my husband took control of it all.

Since then, I've heard that some people on social media thought we were heartless in allowing this kind person to clean up the bloody scene. Our own domestic was as shaken up as we were. I would have done it myself, but the police officers and Emergency Medical Technician recommended that someone completely divorced from the situation should take on that responsibility.

My heartfelt thanks to you Gavin, your family and your domestic for doing this for us. Your act of kindness will never be forgotten.

My husband and his friend, Gavin, came inside hurriedly and told us that a television crew were filming outside the house. I was given strict instructions not to go onto the balcony or outside our home because I'd face a frenzy of journalists.

My husband had called our eldest daughter's partner, Leo, asking him to tell her what had happened and to come through to our home. Leo couldn't come along for support, as our grandson was barely a month old. When I think about this now, it brings tears to my eyes and pain so excruciating words cannot describe it. Had we not survived this home invasion, we might never have known our beautiful grandson, my champ.

When our eldest daughter arrived, I was finally able to take a solitary deep breath. My husband and I and our two daughters clung to each other, weeping, repeating "I love you." One or more of us might not have survived.

We were alive — and it was real.

oooOooo

By this time, the police had converged around our dining room table, I was unmindful of what their discussions entailed. Whilst some of them were going up to the bedroom to gather more evidence, I was sitting in a daze, and it took time for me to realize that one of my sisters' had arrived. She held me close, and I saw the relief in her eyes. She was visibly shaken and concerned for us all.

Earlier that morning, she'd heard what happened and dropped everything to drive through from the East rand. I don't believe for a moment her drive was an easy one. No doubt there was concern all the way. She hadn't spoken to any of us and had no idea what to expect on her arrival. Thank you for your love and care, Linda.

In my confused state, I was approached by a female police officer who asked to take my statement — *in a quiet place*. I excused myself from the collection of concerned friends and family and looked lovingly at my two girls whilst holding a hand of each. Without a word, our eyes met conveying the love between us. At that moment, I realized that my earlier actions or statements could put me behind prison bars.

I now had to face the unknown. I retreated to the kitchen with the female police officer and sat with my feet squarely on the floor, my hands cupped between my thighs. In a daze, I watched her take out her notepad and pen as she detailed the paper with my name and other personal information. Time was pitiful and slow. It felt like hours had passed. I was anxious and overwhelmed with what had happened and what was about to happen. My mind was constantly on my husband and my daughters.

She proceeded with the statement, perhaps a paragraph or so, then one of her superiors approached us and requested that she stop because my trauma was so apparent. She neatly packed her writing tools away, and I re-joined my daughters who were overwhelmingly concerned for me at that point.

I was advised to see my doctor and told that they would return to take my statement when I was less shaken.

A little later, the top police brass arrived. Some of his colleagues updated him on the situation, he then introduced himself and apologized for the trauma we'd endured. He looked me squarely in the eye and shook my hand. *"What a brave decision you made! Certainly, not an easy one, but brave nonetheless. Thank you, on behalf of the police, thank you."* He continued shaking my hand as though we were equal partners. *"From what we have seen at this point, it seems you acted in self-defence."*

He was a kind man. No doubt a hard man, but a kind man.

I couldn't understand any of this. By no means had it minimalized the truth that at some point, I might see the inside of a jail cell, but at that moment, I concentrated on the comfort of having both my daughters and my husband alive and by my side.

I was approached by two more police officers who requested that I hand over both my firearm and my license. I produced them from my bag. My magazine was out, the way I usually kept it – only a single bullet remained. They took them to the table where they had congregated to complete their documentation and eventually bagged my firearm as evidence. My license was returned to me, and I was informed that they required the firearm for further evidence and to analyze whether it had been utilized in any other crime, which was standard procedure.

oooOooo

As a child, my father (now deceased) taught me to aim and shoot pegs off a washing line on our farm, so I've always been familiar with firearms. I acquired my own firearm many years ago when my husband was working away from home for months at a time, and I needed some kind of protection for my girls and me. When it wasn't on my person, it was in my safe — that was my rule. I was very safety conscious, not just because I had two daughters, but because a firearm is not a toy as some people may think. The owner is responsible and needs to use restraint.

Before this particular invasion, my husband and I had been robbed twice before.

During the first robbery, our safe was torn from the wall, and my firearm was amongst the valuables stolen (uninsured, of course).

That incident was reported and given a case number. Police officers came to our home with a fingerprint analyst to investigate. The blue gloves I wore while baking had been taken from my kitchen cupboard and were used during the robbery, some of them found randomly lying about the house. So, we were surprised to learn that they'd found thirty-odd fingerprints. We also noticed shoe prints in some areas of the house, but at the time, the police didn't think those would be of any use, so no prints were taken. I was asked for a detailed list of everything that had been in the safe. Unfortunately, most of the jewellery was never recovered. A suspect was arrested and detained at one point but never convicted. My firearm was returned to me after ballistic tests were completed.

oooOooo

In the later part of the afternoon, after the police, EMT, and coroner left our home, my husband, our younger daughter (who was taking a gap year at the time), and I packed our essentials and left home, little knowing where the journey would take us.

Oddly, I'd decided to take a bath in my daughter's bathroom the night before and left my yellow gold chain and cross beside the tub, thinking I'd retrieve them the following morning. It was important to me, so after all the investigators left, I went to the bathroom to collect it, but, to my dismay, it was gone. As preposterous as this may sound, the only people who went through our house freely and unescorted were the police and investigators.

This was our home we were leaving behind. These were our memories behind brick and mortar.

Eight – A Year in Oblivion

My husband arranged for us to spend a few days away from our home in Johannesburg.

During the first few nights away from our home, I distinctly recall my husband calling me to watch the news channel. To my dismay, right there in front of me I witnessed the presenter relaying our story on national TV. I was in shock and all I could do was sit on the floor and weep.

I was anxious all the time, smoking non-stop, trying to contain and absorb everything that had happened. Tears flowed intermittently. I was in fear all the time, concerned that my eventual statement would land me behind bars and my daughters would have a mother labelled a criminal.

We were staying in a familiar space, but I didn't let my husband or our younger daughter out of my sight. Even going to the bathroom, I couldn't be alone. I clung to my husband twenty-four-seven.

I tried to continue as I always had, but everyday life had become very different and much more difficult. My life had become a foreign place. Every moment of every day and every thought was pure, unadulterated fear.

Nine – Living with a Partner who has P.T.S.D.

A

A Husband's Perspective – Rocky Da Rocha

My husband was angry. All the time.

He was angry that the intruders had invaded the sanctity of our home with the intention of hurting our family.

Yet he fought like a bull in a ring. And he'll always be my matador!

ooo0ooo

We as human beings have dates in our lives that are of significance and importance and we relate to such dates as celebrated, remorseful or sorrowful episodes in our lives.

On the 27th July 2015 at approximately 04:17am, my life changed forever.

This is the date that until today, I wake up every morning on the precise time or earlier.

The 27th July 2015, is a date that I will never forget because it's a date that we as a family managed to survive a horrific home invasion whilst in our peaceful sleep. I have always called our home a sanctuary.

To survive this ordeal is incomprehensible and as a family of three at the time in our home, we all survived, physically unscathed and we all had different outcomes in years ahead in terms of trauma.

My spouse of thirty five years has suffered the most with this terrible ordeal.

In the first few months after this ordeal, I could see that my wife was different. She couldn't solve any small issues that we had, whilst before she always had ten solutions to a problem/ issue. She was the best listener that I ever came across in my life which was not there anymore.

She could be in a relaxed talkative mood and in an instant she could change to an aggressive mood without any provocation. There was no sparkle in her eyes anymore. I remember going to a wedding with my spouse and recall long-time friends that her eyes were dead, and no sparkle. It made me think and when I looked in her eyes I had to agree with that statement.

My spouse was always in control of her life and to some extent mine as well and always put our family first in all her priorities. Sometimes I discussed complex work issues with her in conversations and most times she gave me such positive answers and advice which I used and told her days later, they actually resolved my work issues. This was not there anymore.

I realized that Edna was not well but only realized this when I told her something the day before and she could not remember the conversation the next day. This at times caused arguments because I knew I had told her.

Our youngest daughter, Shante was testament to some of these discussions and we discussed that there is, "really something wrong with Mom."

Edna had no drive to do anything and was always tired, which was never part of her demeanour. If she had a drive or a bit of positive energy, it was short-lived.

Toddlers have always been attracted to Edna and she always showed a very caring attitude to the children. They love her! Our first grandchild was one month old at the time of the ordeal. Edna had such passion, love and enthusiasm for our first grandchild, but it quickly started dwindling after the ordeal and was a concern to me. To this day, I've always said that Edna is the best wife and the best mother our daughters and I could ever wish for.

I had numerous discussions with our daughters Tania and Shante and they agreed with my sentiments. The love she had for me, our daughters and our grandchild was not there anymore the way know she used to show her love. We knew there was something seriously wrong but we had no idea what it was. She burst into tears for no reason and withdrew like at recluse to her bedroom.

She loved cooking, that stopped and when she did cook, there was no love or passion in the food we were used to. She is an exceptional cook.

I had a few discussions about my situation with close friends and most of them suggested that Edna is suffering from depression, which I, being a very positive person didn't know much about.

After about a year of this continuous mood swings Edna said to me one day when I came back from work, "there is something drastically wrong with me." I asked her what made her make that comment she said she nearly committed suicide that day and doesn't know the reasons why she didn't do it. That raised all the hairs on my body.

I was very worried and concerned and after two weeks I confided in one or two close friends regarding what had transpired and one of them came back to me after discussing this with his wife and his wife recommend a psychologist in Cape Town who might be able to help Edna.

After discussing this with Edna she agreed she needed help and our long walk to recovery started.

I was always the type of person that didn't believe in depression, psychologists or psychiatrists and always thought that human beings with mental issues were the ones that needed these services. To this date Edna has both a psychologist and psychiatrist. Over the years I can only thank these two professionals who helped Edna on her path to recovery.

The road ahead was long and difficult but as time passed I could see small improvements, some took months, some took weeks and some were daily.

I will never have the same Edna again, but the road to recovery was well worth it.

I wish I could explain, the love she has for our two grandsons, they adore her and they are both very close to her. There is a special bond between them which is unbelievable and truly noticeable. Very special indeed.

There are still moments that fear does creep in with Edna but I can see she handles it much better than before. She now sometimes is able to give me great advice and solutions like before.

Edna has healed in leaps and bounds. I know it will never be 100 percent the same, but Edna in my view is much closer to that ideal number than before.

Ten – Living with a Mother who has P.T.S.D.

A Daughter's Perspective – Shante Da Rocha

My darling Angel, I know I've given you an awfully difficult task in asking you to share your experience and emotions on paper. I understand how difficult these past few years have been for us all. The fact that you were there that night hurts me to my core.

Your unfailing support and love is commendable.

Know that I love and respect you and that I feel as though I am the most blessed Mother on earth in that I am still here and able to hear your caring voice and hug you each time I see you.

With love and admiration, Mom.

If I had to describe what living with someone diagnosed with P.T.S.D is like, I would have to say it's a polarizing experience that challenges the sense of reality you've always known. As with P.T.S.D, a single event is all it takes to put someone in this state. The event that significantly impacted my mother's life and started her P.T.S.D journey is also the moment I can distinctly mark the change in who I knew my mother to be, to a person that I didn't know, nor did I know how to help. It's as if my mother was taken from me, yet she remained physically present.

When you are not the person experiencing these intense reactions/ feelings, you never truly understand their experience as much as you try to, nor can you predict which way their mood swings. One day I would find my mother exceptionally happy and willing to face the world, the next day she could only function on autopilot, and on other days she would be emotional at any trigger that you were never aware of. My mother's life became more hinged on being aware of threats and that anxiety can trickle down to those closest to them. Unfortunately, her emotions became mine as my protectiveness over her grew. Still, I had to make a clear distinction along her journey that I cannot rectify the wrongs she has experienced or change how the world perceives her or her perception of the world. One thing I realized along her journey was she didn't need solutions from me but rather, she needed someone to listen when she was ready to talk or needed company to make her reality feel like home again.

The P.T.S.D. journey is long and unpredictable one. For the people who have chosen to help those going through P.T.S.D, you need to be okay with walking steadily along the path with them, on other days you need to be okay with not raising a point further because their peace of mind is more important than trying to rehash things, and on the overwhelming days, you are allowed to take moments for you and your life. Although no day is the same and things may not return to your old "reality," you find your new routine and eventually, there are more smiles than tears.

"Mom, no matter the day I will always be here for you to support and love you in ways I am still learning how to."

Eleven – Living with a Mother who has P.T.S.D.

A Daughter's Perspective -Tania Morais (nee Da Rocha)

Almost eight years ago, my family faced a traumatic situation, which has become known as the "incident," and defined a pivotal moment in our lives. Most things are referred to as happening before or after the "incident."

Knowing someone who's survived a traumatic incident is like having a glass jar filled with fireflies. You appreciate the beauty of their light and become mesmerized by their glow, but eventually, they will suffocate from the lack of oxygen, and the light will flicker its last and glow no more. If the gravity of their plight is realized in time, the jar can be opened to set them free.

In this analogy, both my parents and my sister are the fireflies, each entrapped within their own glass jar. My dad and sister have managed to open their jars and fly free, but my mom is still trapped within hers.

Just after the "incident" occurred, my mom began the journey of dissecting the situation, analyzing it piece by piece and unpacking her feelings about the enormity of it all: what happened, why it happened, what could have been done differently, why her, why them, whether it might have resulted in a different outcome, why we deserved to live and not them. Did they have a family? The "incident" had become a glass jar.

My family packed their essential belongings, left the place they used to call home, and moved into an apartment I owned. As time elapsed, my mom's glow and zest for life began to fade. Some of the changes were instant, others were gradual. Normal tasks became tiresome chores. She stopped looking after herself, stopped sleeping, stopped

38

eating, didn't want to leave the apartment, mistrusted everyone, and began carrying her firearm with her wherever she went. She could see the life she wanted outside her jar but had no way of opening it. Over time, her jar became foggy, and she was diagnosed with P.T.S.D.

The doctors prescribed medication to help her process her emotions surrounding the incident. Getting the mix right took months. Some medications made her nauseous, others messed with her sleep. If she forgot to take the meds at the right time, the rest of her day (if not days) was spent in tears she couldn't explain.

A so-called "normal" family gathering, like watching a movie together, had to be carefully censored. My mom couldn't watch anything that contained firearms or violence because it would hit her reset button, making her relive the incident, which would force her to take more meds to deal with the resulting anxiety, and the meds more often than not, would make her drowsy.

She stopped driving altogether, so she was unable to do simple tasks, to collect the post, buy groceries, and so on. She became a hermit, entirely dependent on my dad to get to places. It took her a few years to gather enough courage to climb into her car and drive fifteen minutes to visit me, and when she reached me, she had to take anxiety meds to calm her nerves before she could drive back.

When I was younger, my mom loved cooking and made wholesome, tasty meals I still crave. After the "incident," she stopped cooking entirely. Again, it took a few years before she felt comfortable enough to cook a meal. Slowly, she was able to cook another meal, then another.

Such ordinary daily tasks, which we take for granted, were an achievement for my mom. She had lost her way, and it took great effort to accomplish small tasks. We celebrated the small wins. She wanted to make progress, but it seemed she was always taking steps backward, feeling that everything was out of her control.

Over the years, there has been a constant debate about if the house where the "incident" occurred should be sold so that my parents could move forward with their lives or if they should move back to what was once their home. They had been without a home for so long, and they were missing it. Their items were scattered amongst different residences. They felt they weren't ready to sell the house, but it was still filled with triggers for my mom. Her doctors advised against it, saying that moving back could wipe out the progress she'd made. My parents had increased the security there, installing alarms, beams, electric fences, cameras, and shutter doors to close off the living space from the rest of the house. In the seventh year after the incident, they took the leap and decided to give it another chance, to live at home. I often ask myself whether a house that looks like a prison can still be a home. I hope so for my parent's sake, but only time will tell.

The problem with being stuck in a glass jar is that no one can open it for you. You alone need to walk the path, process the emotions, know what you want for your life, grasp it with both hands, and have the motivation and energy to move forward. As her daughter, I often feel helpless in this situation. Although the solution is simple, the fact that I wasn't in the house when the incident occurred makes me an outsider. I don't fully understand what it's like to live with P.T.S.D. and cannot fathom why opening a glass jar is so difficult. I have confidence in my mom and her progress, and I know she can move forward if she accepts the past for what it is, knowing it's no longer within her control, and focus her energy on the path that lies ahead. By no means will it be easy, but she can decide what her future should look like and move in that direction.

Mom, I will always be here for you in any way you need. You are stronger than you let yourself believe. The unfortunate reality is that in a split second, you had to make the decision to protect the family, despite the cost to your emotional well-being. If you hadn't, I wouldn't have my parents and my sister with me today, and my sons wouldn't know my side of the family.

Keep taking steps forward, even if they may seem small. Surround yourself with positivity and things that make you happy. When you're ready, you'll be able to open the glass jar!

Twelve – Anxiety, Depression, and Medical Help

This "thing," this Post Traumatic Stress Disorder has been extremely difficult for me to accept.

About a year after the invasion, I still felt that my world had been turned upside down and inside out. Nothing made sense anymore, I couldn't make heads or tails of my day or where I was. For no reason whatsoever, I was plagued with constant exhaustion and migraine headaches. I quietly lived through the constant pain that filtered to my arms and chest.

After attempting to deal with these issues on my own, not wanting to add additional strain on my husband, I told him there was something desperately wrong with me, but I couldn't articulate exactly what it was. I needed help. I wasn't sure what kind of help I needed, but I think he understood. I'd never been one to complain, but persevered and sought a solution myself.

He told me that he'd spoken to a lot of people about the home invasion, and a friend in Cape Town had recommended a psychologist. He was wonderful in securing an appointment, and before I knew it, we were on a plane to Cape Town.

As neither of us wanted to uproot our youngest daughter again, we arranged for her to stay with her older sister who had recently finished building a new home with her partner. At the time of the incident, their son had been barely a month old.

During the flight, I was anxious. I looked out the window and prayed, tears streaming down my face. I was so embarrassed I couldn't look the flight attendant in the eye. I didn't want to speak to anyone. I wanted to be left alone. I wanted to hide. I didn't understand how I was feeling or why, at a moment's notice, I would become emotional and tears would fill my eyes. During the past year, I'd cried very often. I could make no sense of my feelings or emotions, which seemed beyond my control. I was afraid of everything and only felt safe when my husband was within sight.

This thing I'm going through and suffering with; this Post Traumatic Stress Disorder, has been and to some extent still is extremely difficult for me to accept.

I've never get sick easily, and I've always been tough on myself, putting others first without considering my own well-being — perhaps because I got so much joy from pleasing others. But for eight years since the incident, nothing could bring a smile to my face.

My psychologist, Dr. Gary Read had often asked asked how I felt, and there came a point when I realized I was dead inside. No feelings, no anger, no hate — just dead.

I'd never taken medicine regularly, but now I was bombarded with it. I don't know what I expected, but I felt it made no difference at all. I literally handed my life to my psychologist, Dr. Gary Read, and my psychiatrist, Dr. Christine Tomcheck.

I had no sense nor purpose. It took months and, in some instances, years to find the exact combination of medicines that would help me. I was physically ill, night and day because of the foreign substances my body had to deal with. I had no idea what to expect and went into this blindly. I tried desperately to hang on and trust my doctors without knowing they'd eventually help me through my anxiety and fear.

I avoided people at all costs, I clung to my husband's arm, and couldn't lift my head. I was afraid that the assailants who got away would recognize us. I was a nervous wreck, constantly surveying where we were, looking for an escape route. I couldn't go anywhere near crowds, and I frequently lost control of my breathing and collapsed. I avoided all the things regular people do and became a recluse, though I didn't know it at the time.

My nights were equally frightening. At night the fear of shutting down enveloped me. I was afraid of closing my eyes and seeing the intruder standing over me and fighting me on the bed. I was afraid of having to fire a bullet. Afraid for my family. The nightmares and flashbacks didn't stop. I relived each moment of our ordeal over and over.

For me it had now become the survival of my mind.

I was in a daze each and every day. I began having trouble remembering which medication to take at what time and had to be reminded by my family. I hated it. I hated putting those indelicate pills down my throat several times a day just to get by. I battled to swallow most of the medications, which seemed to get stuck in my throat.

At times, I ran to the bathroom heaving and hurling for minutes on end. After two years of taking the medications, I realized I needed to write down when I should be taking each one on the packet and on a note stuck on the fridge, and put a tick next to it when I took it. Our younger daughter helped by setting alarms on my cell phone to remind me because I couldn't remember how to do that simple task myself. In some ways, my mind had been reduced to that of a child.

Days turned into months and months into years. It has been several years since the home invasion, but I still think about it often.

During the infrequent times when I thought I was strong enough to accompany my family to breakfast, people would speak to my husband or send messages saying how *strong* I was, or refer to me as a *hero*, or say they didn't know anyone who would have been able to do what I did. None of that mattered to me. No one knew what I was going through. No-one knew what I was harbouring inside; my thoughts, my hurt, my pain. No one thought about how I had to deal with breaking one of the Ten Commandments. It was all me ... me alone.

I couldn't see past the next minute, so planning anything was difficult.

This person wasn't me. I'd become someone I didn't recognize, someone totally oblivious to life passing her by.

Within a year of being on the medication, I'd gained ten kilograms, too much for a small-boned person with hereditary polycystic kidney disease. The additional weight put tremendous strain on my lower back and there were times I couldn't distinguish what made me more ill. Everything became a blur. One day was followed by the next, only to be repeated once more. Every night was hell, filled with flashbacks. I didn't want to go to bed fearing the terror would strike again.

Each morning, I woke with bruises on my arms and legs. Dr. Read surmised that in my sleep, I was reliving the incident, harming myself in the process. My psychiatrist prescribed additional medication before bed to still my mind. It took years for me to slowly stop harming myself as I slept.

oooOooo

My weekly sessions with Dr. Read were conducted remotely, and from time to time, I flew to Cape Town to see him and my psychiatrist, Dr. Tomcheck.

I was never someone who shared things easily, never a talker, really, especially about my feelings or experiences. I was a private person. During many sessions, I had next to nothing to say and sat quietly, listening, feeling anxious, and not understanding what I was going through. I don't recall much of those initial sessions. And I say *initial* loosely since it's been several years.

I cried often, feeling pain I wouldn't wish on my worst enemy. I was hurting for my family. I was hurting for the intruders' families, and for myself. I had taken two lives, broken one of God's commandments – the very belief that made me who I am.

I couldn't shut down. I was afraid to fall asleep, and when the medication eventually took effect, I'd wake up in a cold sweat, screaming and crying, reliving the incident all over again, thinking I was in that bedroom with that man pushing me back down onto the bed. Nightmares and flashbacks became regular visitors.

I was always on high alert, vulnerable, hurting, and crying convulsively. Thoughts of taking my own life were my constant companions.

oooOooo

Our eldest daughter graciously let us stay in her apartment in Bedfordview. *No need to pay us Mom, please just get better.* I cried frequently, wondering how this daughter of mine could be so kind when she could have received a rental income. I was riddled with guilt, trying to come to grips with my situation.

I lacked the energy and inclination to do the grocery shopping. I completely stopped cooking or baking, which I'd loved and taken pride in. I stopped doing photography altogether.

I desperately needed just a moment's rest, a moment when it would all go away. But it seemed life had other plans for me. Closing my eyes, even for a brief moment, instantly brought flashbacks.

Those days were so dark and so deep I thought I would never recover. I couldn't see the light. Twice, I took my firearm from the safe and put it on the bed beside me, thinking they should have killed me that night. I was numb and confused, wondering how I could live like that, unable to see past the next moment, each day darker than the day before. Twice, I lifted the firearm to put it to my head, thinking that it would just take a moment. Silence was all around me. My hands were shaking uncontrollably, tears finding their way down my cheeks as I held that piece of metal in my hands, lifted it, and for a moment, I closed my eyes and thought about my youngest daughter. Did I want to put her through more pain? Did I want her to find me lying in a pool of blood when she came home? I lowered the firearm, crying uncontrollably, praying as I have never prayed before. I was drained and so very, very tired.

I realize now that the burden I carried was enormous. There was no end in sight. The light at the end of the tunnel had gone out. My flame for life extinguished.

I rarely answered my phone. Sometimes, I replied to a message from a friend or family member. I was sent an inspiring message every day without fail, but no one needed to know how I felt. I'd always been so strong, no burden was too heavy to carry. Why couldn't I get up and dust myself off this time? It wasn't through a lack of trying. Living had become an insurmountable task.

Doing something small was difficult enough, but without warning, something reminded me of the incident. It could be an innocuous noise or a fleeting vision. The anxiety was exponential. I'd suddenly be in a state of shock, followed by uncontrollable shaking so severe I couldn't light a cigarette. I cowered at the slightest sound. Although I spent most of my time in the small apartment, I was always looking for an escape route. I needed to get out, to get away from the noise. I'd fall into a little huddle, tears covering my face, closing my eyes, wishing it would stop.

It didn't. Not for a long time. Even now, many years after the incident, I still feel that way at times. Though I'm awfully aware of what I do and where I go – anxiety still lingers close behind.

I stopped driving. I knew I wouldn't be able to handle the responsibility or the noise on the roads. I wouldn't be able to cope with all the vehicles, cars moving from one lane to another. The anxiety came on quickly, and it took a long time for me to return to a neutral state. I became weaker and more depressed.

Perhaps I wanted to keep pretending everything was all right. But it wasn't.

My breathing became heavy and quick. The pains down my arms and into my chest increased. When I rode in the car as a passenger, I had to open the aircon vents and inhale the cold air until my shaking lessened to a bearable level. I couldn't see a way out, and I felt trapped, exhausted and numb. I focused on taking that next breath, holding my clenched fist against my breastbone to ease the pain.

Days turned into months; and months into years.

My bedroom, my sanctuary had been invaded. What was I to do? I was lost.

It was clear to all around me that depression had hit me like a head on collision.

It is more than eight years since the incident and I still think about it and how it affects my every thought, my every action. Each moment of the day and every thought is one of pure unadulterated fear!

Thirteen – A Message to the Home Invaders

To you who came into our home uninvited, and to your family who probably knew what you did for a so-called-living:

Whoever you are, wherever you are, know that you have not only ruined my life but have disrupted my family's life, as well.

All these years, I've been living with the guilt of having taken the lives of two men while defending my family. But YOU, yes YOU, the other people who were on our property! I hope you read this someday and know you have taken my spirit for living, my joy in family, the essence of my everyday existence.

I hope you can live with that.

And I pray that your sons and daughters never follow in your footsteps.

Fourteen – Year Twenty-Twenty

A peculiar year, to say the least. On the surface, we all experienced changes and difficulties during this time of COVID, which affected everyone's lives in a way our world had never seen.

Packing, stocking up, and ensuring all family members were in a safe place are but a few of the obstacles people worldwide had to embrace. Lockdown became a very real thing.

We were blessed that at least some members of our family were together. Being away from loved ones; as I'm sure many millions of people know, pulls at the heartstrings. Knowing there will be no visits, no hugs, no laughter, or joy for many months to come.

We were only allowed to leave home to purchase my monthly medication, and even then, we had to show the doctor's scripts and carry identification. I had never seen the roads so empty of cars, but police were everywhere.

During this time, Mother Nature found a way to recover from a little of the damage we humans have inflicted. Weather patterns changed. The waters were cleaner. A dolphin was seen swimming in the canals of Venice. Who would have thought? Roads were cleaner and violent crimes were fewer. The sale of black-market cigarettes and alcohol increased.

After lockdown, when movement was unrestricted again, I realized how it had affected my P.T.S.D.

When the time came for my husband to go back to his office, I had to force myself to purchase our groceries on my own. I didn't mind wearing a mask, but I realized that when I saw an oncoming non-white figure, my anxiety kicked in. I often felt dizzy, gasped for air, and held onto a wall for fear of collapsing. The overwhelming feeling of needing to escape ensued. Often, I'd abandon my shopping and go back up the lift, hoping I wouldn't have to share the elevator space with strangers.

I was gripped with the fear of encountering a black male wearing a black mask, reminding me of the balaclavas the intruders wore. The fear was so overwhelming, I needed additional medication to relieve the anxiety.

The masks were a constant reminder of the incident. My family had to change the colour of masks worn in my presence. If I met someone wearing a dark coloured or black mask, I avoided their eyes and focused on the floor. To this day, it disturbs me.

Fifteen – That Night, 27th July 2015

Written 28th November 2019

As they entered the bedroom, I sat upright in bed. There were two of them. I grabbed my firearm from my bag beside my bed and pushed in the magazine. Within seconds, I realized someone was forcefully gripping both my arms and pushing me down onto the bed. My arms were being pried apart.

I looked over at my husband. He had already reached the foot of the bed when I saw the firearm held in both the intruder's hands pointing directly at him. My husband was desperately trying to push the firearm away from his face. Instinctively, I knew I had to fight. I needed to find the strength to bring my arms together so I could cock my own firearm. Somewhere from within I found a surge of strength. I was still being pushed down onto the bed with beastly strength.

My mind was racing everywhere at once. *Rocky has to overcome the other intruder … I need to get to my daughter … Is someone in her room already?* They needed me, and they needed me now! I had one chance only. Just one! My decision had to be quick and on point. I had to let the assailant lean in a little closer so my firearm was in direct contact with his body. I couldn't falter. I felt his weight. I smelled his acrid odour.

I cocked my pistol and pulled the trigger.

A flash of light emitted from the barrel in our dark bedroom. I felt the sudden release of pressure on my arms. In shock, I watched the masked intruder stagger backward and collapse on the floor, face up, arms outspread, his firearm still in the palm of his hand.

My husband was struggling to hold off the second intruder. "Hold him!" I yelled and scrambled over the back of the bed, my firearm at the ready lest a third person was in our daughter's bedroom. That moment was one of complete understanding between the two of us. I ran to check on my daughter who had been awakened by the commotion. "Lock your door, my angel, and don't come out until you hear my voice." I heard the click of the key. Every sound pronounced.

I ran back to our bedroom. By this time, my husband had managed to wrestle the second intruder through the sliding door to the far end of the balcony.

As I ran back to them, I heard a voice from the street screaming in panic, "Rocky are you okay?" It was our neighbour. We yelled back, "Call the police!" My husband was on his knees, struggling to gain control of the intruder's firearm to keep the barrel from pointing at his head. The second intruder had noticed me and had pushed me with his full body weight against the glass door. I stumbled, slightly dazed from knocking my head against the glass. I had to recover quickly, nothing else mattered. Holding my firearm in both my hands to steady myself, I prayed to our Lord above, *Please God, let me not harm my husband.* I got as close to the intruder as I could and fired. The shot resounded, and I watched him stumble back towards the balustrade as though he were trying to escape and fling his body over the balcony.

In shock, I looked at my husband. My mind was already on the safety of our daughter, and I ran back into our bedroom to make sure the first intruder was unable to do us further harm. I had to remind myself to breathe. He was lying motionless on the floor, so I ran to my daughter's room and called through her locked door. She called back that she was okay, but I reminded her not to open the door until I came back.

I collected my keys and opened the shutters to the lower level, all the while pointing my firearm and hoping I wouldn't encounter another intruder. By this time, Rocky had called our armed response guard. When I reached the ground level, he was outside our gate. We both saw that intruder who had leapt from the balcony and was lying spread-eagled at our front door. A shudder ran down my spine, and I gasped for air at the shock of his lifeless body.

Our armed guard continued searching for more intruders while I ran back upstairs to my husband and daughter on the top floor. We all silently thanked God that He had held us safely in His hands that night.

Without a word passing between us, we knew that God had afforded us a miracle.

Sixteen – Day-to-Day Experiences

22^(nd) January 2016

We'd moved into my eldest daughter's apartment, away from the house where the incident occurred, but that day, I was back at the house, packing a few items and babysitting our grandson. Whilst putting him to sleep, I briefly closed my eyes, and the strangest of feelings passed through my body. Was this a reminder of what had happened the year before? Was this telling me I shouldn't be there? I was deeply afraid. The incident kept recurring in my mind. I picked up my grandson and left the bedroom.

After my grandson went home with my daughter, I tried again to find peace in the bedroom where the incident took place. But when I lay down, the same strange, dark feeling passed through my body.

Two days later, when I mentioned it to my husband, he told me that he'd had a similar feeling at the house a few weeks before.

I knew then that a priest would have to be brought to our home where we'd been so content and cleanse the dark feelings we'd both experienced.

25^(th) January 2016

It dawned on me that I might never be able to move back to our home.

My husband frequently had to travel for business, and I was afraid of being alone. I was disappointed that he was leaving me again so soon.

11^(th) April 2016 (Cape Town)

I cannot think of a better word than just feeling *lost*.

12^(th) April 2016 (Cape Town)

I'm becoming afraid at the thought of continuing to renovate our home, still feeling lost and so very lonely with only my emotions to keep me company.

Psalm 51 – A Prayer for Forgiveness
Be merciful to me, oh God,
Because of your constant love.
Because of your great mercy wipe away my sins!
Wash away all my evil and make me clean from my sin!
I recognize my faults; I am always conscious of my sins.
I have sinned against you –
Only against you –
And done what you consider evil.
So you are right in judging me; you are justified in condemning me.
I have been evil from the day I was born; from the time I was conceived,
I have been sinful.
Sincerity and truth are what you require; fill my mind with your
wisdom.
Remove my sin, and I will be clean; wash me, and
I will be whiter than snow.
Let me hear the sounds of joy and gladness.
And though you have crushed me and broken me,
I will be happy once again.
Close your eyes to my sins and wipe out all my evil.
Create a pure heart in me, O God, and put a new and loyal spirit in me.
Do not banish me from your presence;
Do not take your holy spirit from your salvation,
And make me willing to obey you.
Then I will teach sinners your commands,
And they will turn back to you.
Spare my life, O God, and save me, and I will gladly proclaim your
righteousness.
Help me speak, Lord, and I will praise you.
You do not want sacrifices, or I would offer them;
You are not pleased with burnt-offerings.
My sacrifice is a humble spirit, O God;

You will not reject a humble and repentant heart.
O God, be kind to Zion and help her,
Rebuild the walls of Jerusalem.
Then you will be pleased with proper sacrifices
And burnt-offerings; and bulls will be sacrificed on your altar.

13th April 2016 (Cape Town)

I need to be released from this jail in my head. I need to get away for a time, and do some kind of activity that would push me to the limits with resolute danger.

I'm plagued with feelings of insecurity and unsure whether I should call my psychologist. I've heard of people going through such profound trauma that the guilt of surviving becomes too much to endure. I know that I am deliberating with myself whether this may be me right now.

I do so want to feel empowered again!

18th April 2016

Many thoughts are racing through my mind, and I have mixed feelings about our house. I'm crying all the time, desperately trying to get to the next step of healing, but at the same time, I really want to finish the renovations we started. I feel my husband is unwittingly adding additional pressure because his work constantly takes him away from me, and I'm often overcome by feelings of being alone and abandoned when what I need most is comfort.

I'm so confused. I'm afraid of going back to the house and sleeping in that room. I'm afraid my husband will have to leave on business at a moment's notice, and I'll be left alone again. I DON'T HAVE THE STRENGTH TO DO IT!

I keep asking myself, *Am I expecting too much of myself or my loved one's?*

19th April 2016 (Bedfordview)

"Lord, if it's Your will, let this pain slip from my grasp and give me peace not to worry."

Faith is the first step. Even if you can't see the stairway at present.

I yearn to know what it feels like to have a real smile on my face again.

21st April 2016

A Note from a Mother to her Angels, Tania and Shante:
I gave birth to you, yet you came with no instructions. All I knew was that I loved you long before I saw you. I made mistakes along the way, and I am sorry, but I did the best I could with what I knew."

Everything I did, I did with love. You are my child, my life, and my dreams for tomorrow. I will always love you, and nothing could ever destroy that love."

25th April 2016
To those who coveted my life:
Think carefully and choose wisely, as you will have to walk a day in my shoes and experience my deepest, darkest, most degrading moments. Some days are even too much for me to get through.

29th April 2016
From the age of six to nine months, my grandson spent each day with me. I loved the company, and at the time, I thought it would be a diversion from my P.T.S.D. insanity.

One day when my spirits were especially low, I was playing games with him in his cot, and I suddenly began crying softly. He looked up at me with both love and concern in those beautiful expressive eyes, reached up, and gently held my hand. I cannot explain the bond I felt right there, right then.

I know that on the night of the incident, a true miracle was performed. What I don't yet understand is why I survived. I'm truly grappling with that idea. *"Please Lord, I beg You, help me find the answer."*

10th May 2016
Today my husband took me to collect my so-called certificate of appreciation, awarded by the South African Police Department for bravery as a woman. I was hurting and apprehensive and had declined an invitation to a breakfast for the honourees. I didn't feel that being

awarded for taking the lives of two men would in any way relieve my P.T.S.D., and I didn't want to attract attention to myself.

As time went by, I knew that going to the police station to collect the certificate would be a positive step in my healing.

16th May 2016
DESPONDENT!

27 July 2016

It's been exactly one year since the incident, so my husband and I decided to go to a small nearby chapel. As we entered, we took each other's hands and found an empty pew where we kneeled together. I clasped my hands and prayed desperately for forgiveness, crying uncontrollably all the while. I can't say how long I was there. I prayed for the souls of the deceased. I prayed for their families. I prayed for their forgiveness, and I thanked the Lord that our family made it through this ordeal.

I still feel the deepest guilt for having taken the lives of those two men whose names I never knew. I still think of them as *"someone's son, someone's husband* and *someone's father,* and it rips my heart apart.

When we finished our prayer, my husband and I each lit a candle and left the chapel, then stood for a while, looking out at the garden, breathing the cool winter air. For a brief moment, I smelled the scent of roses, but looking around there was not a single rose in sight. I asked my husband if he could smell the roses, and he shook his head. Was this my pardon? My release? Relief from my burden?

January 2017

During the time I spent in Cape Town with our youngest daughter, I decided to get a tattoo. I've never liked tattoos, nor did I want to defile my body with ink. But this day, I decided to get not one, but two tattoos. I had a cross engraved on the nape of my neck and the other, just two simple words CARPE DIEM – seize the day, on my left wrist. To me, they represented my religion and my survival. A daily reminder.

As time progressed, the mental anguish also became physical. The recurring nightmares and flashbacks left me drained and lethargic. At times, my husband's relentless anger at the invaders frightened me, and every day he discussed the invasion, adding more strain. I felt I was spiralling into a deeper depression. At some point, it occurred to me that we were slowly drifting apart. He was living in anger, and I was living in pain.

23rd March 2017

Mercy has become my only door to freedom.

7th April 2017

Words of wisdom and encouragement from my psychologist, Dr. Gary Read: *Let's just keep on walking ... we'll get through this together.* Whether I realized it at the time or not, it felt good to know I had the support.

13th April 2017

I've been told that some trauma survivors find the guilt too much to bear. This may be true of me, sitting on the precipice of insanity. I often feel I've been emotionally violated.

20th April 2017

I have a constant nagging feeling. I'm low and defeated, drained and lethargic.

22nd April 2017

Another visit to our house today. I brought sage and a white candle to cleanse the house. My husband and I did this together, both hoping the peace and calm would return. I was disappointed in myself as I couldn't enter the bedroom. That will have to wait for another day.

23rd April 2017

Went again to the house to cleanse it. My husband and I read a cleansing prayer together. Another emotional struggle to overcome my dread of entering the bedroom.

Like the hands of a clock turned back in time, it all came flooding back. The visuals, the feeling of being pressed down onto the bed, my finger pulling down on the trigger, not once but twice, and the collapse of two strange men. The shock, the panic, the guilt.

May 2017

During this time of turmoil, I declined many invitations from family and friends. Not everyone understood that my refusal was not aimed at hurting them, but a reaction to the anxiety and depression I was suffering. My psychologist explained to me that for those who have not experienced P.T.S.D. it would be incredibly difficult for them to understand it.

6th June 2017

There comes a time when you realize that you must do this on your own. You must take it day by day and sometimes it's just simply hour by hour.

Often people would express their empathy and concern, and then continue with their daily lives.

You're the one who must claw your way through these emotions, these very painful and damaging reminders.

I have come to realize that this is the reality of Post-Traumatic Stress Disorder.

18th July 2017

I lost interest in my business, and it suffered. I had to cancel all existing contracts. I stopped caring. Eventually, I closed my business. My family suffered. I was in an indescribable place. Surreal? I'm not sure. But I was lost.

Each and every day was torture.

I had taken the lives of two people, and all I wanted to do lay down, close my eyes and disappear.

I hated myself. Some days, I still do. My mind is permanently on high alert. I still struggle at the sight of a firearm or balaclava's, even if it's only in a movie, even if someone mentions it in a conversation.

And I wonder if this will go on forever.

24th July 2017

My husband told me that our youngest daughter, who was in the house the night of the incident, mentioned that she's been suffering from nightmares.

The affect this has had on my family is unbearable. I have to keep reminding myself that if there had been another option, I would have taken it. My daughter didn't mention it to me, but I found out later that she didn't want to add additional pressure on me. In time we arranged sessions for her with my psychologist. But still, I could not free myself of the thought that she must have been so afraid; so alone not knowing what was happening.

I feel dreadful. I'm meant to be there for my daughter as a mother, not the other way around.

I feel guilty that she is so concerned about my mental and physical health, especially now that she's away at university.

6th August 2017

I'm still experiencing awful nightmares. I wake up in a cold sweat with bruises all over my body.

11th October 2017

My husband's been returning from work late at night and I constantly feel alone. The past two years have taken a toll on us all.

12th October 2017

I regret that I survived our ordeal.

I'm not living. I'm simply surviving.

27th October 2017

I don't have scars on the outside for people to see. My scars lie within, hidden from the world. Is that why no one understands people with P.T.S.D.? Or is it just easier to ignore my pain and carry on?

6th February 2018

I feel I'm slowly making progress, but I still have setbacks, and the lack of sleep is still an ongoing problem.

I miss our home, our freedom, and my happy family.

Again today, I thought about having taken the lives of two people, but I know this is my cross to bear for the rest of my life.

I still battle with unexpected or loud sounds, and with masks or face coverings that remind me of balaclavas.

Even my husband can only understand to a certain point. I still often wonder what happened to the third invader. No case was filed, since it was determined that I acted in self-defence and to save our family.

7th February 2018

Feeling so low again, and the pain in my left arm and chest just won't subside.

22nd February 2018

This week, I saw a story on the Discovery channel about the murder of inventor Nicola Tesla. For the first time, something small became clearer to me, and I realized that during our incident; I had in fact saved three people!

It was a small epiphany.

I made the decision to join a gym. It was difficult for me to go into a public space, because I was constantly aware of and suspicious of those around me. Yet I felt selfish - I didn't deserve to breathe, let alone join a gym. I didn't deserve to do anything because I'd taken two lives, but here my psychologist corrected me on this, and he told me I needed to be self-focused to heal.

I liked that! I had just taken a very bold step.

8th March 2018

In the Bedfordview apartment, it was easy to peer over the balcony onto the square below. I kept noticing families moving into their new apartments, making a home for themselves. That's what I missed, my home. This is my goal and my dream, to experience my home again, the fun and laughter.

It saddens me to say that whilst we moved out of our home, and I was trying to keep a grip on my tumultuous emotions, I realized that both my husband and I were dealing with our own pain separately and very differently, and perhaps we were also silently letting go of our marriage, bit by bit.

When my psychologist asked what I was feeling, my response was rather simple, my feelings were neutral. I didn't care for life. Not people, not where I would be in an hour or even tomorrow. I was dead inside. I was nothing.

I most certainly didn't feel I had the right to want or need a home. I didn't deserve the people who cared for me.

21st March 2018

I went to the house again today to see the progress on the renovations, and I wondered how it would ever be possible to feel at home in the place I have now become most afraid of.

I feel and remember the remnants of my old self on the odd occasion.

10th April 2018

I want to be the phoenix who rises from the ashes of her broken life.

23 June 2018

My husband and I went to Venice to celebrate our thirty-year anniversary. In Venice, I felt somewhat alive again. Safe. A little of my old self was still inside. Even though I was still heavily medicated, being removed from the offending surroundings, I could pause and look at the situation from a different perspective.

I felt so free, so peaceful and full of life.

But back in South Africa, the reality set in, and life became as it was before.

19th July 2018

I've tried to desensitize myself from traumatic triggers by watching a movie or the news. So far, I've not been successful, the sound of a firearm, or the sight of it being in someone's hand or any related violence still escalates my anxiety.

Trying to desensitize myself and failing makes me fear I haven't achieved much these past years. I thought I was ready.

6th August 2018

At times, I equate P.T.S.D to a toddler taking their first steps, slowly and mechanically. Each step, however small, becomes a victory.

13th August 2018

I have come to wonder, without disappointments, how do we measure our lives?

20th August 2018

I've noticed that as a general rule, people who have never suffered with depression or experienced Post-Traumatic Stress Disorder don't have the tools, or lack the understanding to be around people like me.

My immediate family have been very compassionate, caring and patient.

I overheard my eldest daughter, Tania, describing me to my grandson as "a delicate flower." It broke my heart to know that a young boy had to hold himself back playing games, joking, not free to express his joy and happiness for fear of frightening me. Yet her kind consideration has never been lost on me.

In one way or another, this thing has eaten away at every bit of my life.

These are the times when I resent myself the most.

24th August 2018

I came across this quote, which I think describes me exceptionally well at this point in my journey:

If I were a landscape –

I'd be a swamp.
Author Unknown

28th August 2018

The fear is still the same. The flashbacks are incessant and unrelenting.

Any movie that shows a person in a headdress, mask, or balaclava instantly takes me back to the incident. It is tiresomely difficult to even pen this word.

I am constantly on edge and it seems sleeping has become a myth in my world. I am frequently lethargic and confused.

Even after three years, I still wake up in a cold sweat from time to time.

When I was pregnant with our second daughter, I was diagnosed with the hereditary polycystic kidney disease my father had. The deterioration has been slow and has not yet affected my quality of life.

It has been a difficult thing to share with our girls, and I worry about their future and my husband's when it finally takes its toll.

Dear Lord please give them the strength.

1st September 2018

To quote a song sung by Elvis Presley, "Lord, this time you gave me a mountain ..."

4th September 2018

In addition to my Post-Traumatic Stress Disorder and its depressive effects, my thoughts have been flooded with the deterioration of my kidneys. I know I have to be strong for my family and take one day at a time.

12th September 2018

Although I'm in a safe place away from Johannesburg on my own whilst my husband is away for business, I still haven't been sleeping well.

Being on my own, tests my resolve. During the day, I seem to be more comfortable - it's the night time that gets me.

When I look in the mirror, the person looking back has become tired, the eyes weary.

It's odd to feel so empty and worried at the same time.

12th October 2018

I'm back at the house where it all fell apart. I'm alone, sitting in my study, firearm at my side. It's dusty after all these years, and the air smells a little stale.

Everything is exactly where I left it three years ago.

I hope being here will help me progress. I'm bargaining, no, relying on my tenacity.

15TH Aug 2019

I can't have the life I had before the invasion, but I can't give up hope on this version of my life.

21st August 2019

I'M ALIVE ...

1st November 2019

I'm clutching the front of my nightgown as though I'm clutching onto my sanity, holding onto a life that may never happen.

21st November 2019

I've abandoned people. Perhaps I'm just exhausted from this long ordeal.

3rd December 2019

To my daughters: *You girls are my heart, walking on the outside of my body. Love, Mom.*

6th April 2020

Even if I don't emphasize myself or my life, I must emphasize my girls and grandson, I have to focus on the positives in my life.

11th April 2020

Because I believe the Lord is omnipotent, it's difficult to be impressed with the things we humans do or say. I keep asking myself if I still lack emotion, or have I just become cynical? Perhaps it's simply just the state of my tumultuous mind.

20ᵗʰ April 2020

I remember the previous robbery and keep trying to make sense of it. I distinctly remember that the blue gloves I used for baking were taken from my kitchen cupboard.

I remember that all the duplicate keys were removed from the cupboard where I had kept them. They were missing – all of them.

At one point, we were told that one person had been taken into custody, questioned, held for a short while, but never convicted.

1ˢᵗ May 2020

When there is nothing for me to hold onto, God will hold onto me.

18ᵗʰ May 2020

As months and years went by, I experienced frequent bouts of memory loss. The information sounded familiar and triggered a sense of knowing, but I couldn't retrieve the information leaving me frustrated, vulnerable, and embarrassed.

25ᵗʰ May 2020

I came across this saying: "history is written by survivors." Rather apt, I thought. It's uncanny that we must endure pain and the guilt whilst trying to survive.

5ᵗʰ June 2020

I've come to the point where I feel my essence has disappeared along with my zest for life. At times, I wonder at times what the point of living is, what the point of having survived is?

14ᵗʰ June 2020

Then there are times where I feel chipped but not yet broken…

I'm anxious because the anniversary of the invasion is creeping closer.

I must get through this. I must take control of my life. I must stop remembering that date. It's gone. It's over.

Yet I'm afraid to go to sleep, afraid to shut down.

22 June 2020

I'm experiencing memory loss more and more often. No matter how hard I try to remember, things I used to know seem only a little familiar. Whilst everyone around me has wonderful intentions and tells me I'll get back to normal, I know differently. I feel utterly useless — idiotic almost.

At times, I can't recall a simple word or sequence of words in a sentence. I can't remember places we've been as a family. Most of my precious memories are now lost to me.

14th July 2020

One of my sisters mentioned that she still has press coverage of the invasion, which she downloaded from the internet and emailed to me.

I began to read the first page, and the photos brought the incident to the forefront of my mind. I was traumatized, I sat still as a statue for a while, then had to put it all away and out of sight.

15th July 2020

Another of my sisters asked if she could read through those files, and I agreed. But she naively kept asking me questions. I tried my best to answer, until all my emotions came flooding back and I was sobbing again. I asked her to excuse me so I could gather myself and wipe away the tears. Both my psychologist and psychiatrist had suggested that in these instances, I should ask to change the subject. Unfortunately, in these flustered moments, I do not always remember what they had suggested.

I hope that as years go by, the incident will either be forgotten or, at least, become easier to cope with.

16th July 2020

The last two days have set the tone for the anniversary of the incident. I've tried to keep a brave face and kept busy to avoid the thoughts that plague my mind.

19th July 2020

Our eldest daughter had a get-together to celebrate her birthday. I spent a lot of the time away from the others and on my own, outside on the deck, using all my restraint to hold back the tears. I didn't want to dampen such a joyous occasion.

20th July 2020

I had an appointment with the optometrist today and whilst I was trying on new reading glasses, I noticed in the mirror that my lip was drooping on one side again. I wasn't sure whether this was related to my previous stroke, or a sign that another stroke was oncoming. In twenty-eighteen I had been referred to a Neurologist to test whether I had had a stroke. The test result had been positive and it had been concluded that the stroke had been caused by my trauma and anxiety.

20 July 2020

Five years ago, before the incident, we were in the process of renovating our house. When we moved out of our home and into our daughter's apartment, the renovations came to a complete halt.

For a number of years, I couldn't go near the house, and when I finally did, I was heavily medicated. Even so, I couldn't make it past the first floor. Memories of that night were still too vivid. I was overwhelmed and kept looking for an escape. It didn't feel like home anymore.

Since then, I've returned many times, trying to slowly reintroduce myself to each area of the house. Everything I touched or smelled unleashed a memory of *before* the incident. At times, I became physically ill or wept so relentlessly I needed to take additional medication. The triggers overwhelmed me.

Now, five years on, the renovation is slowly taking place again. My psychologist tells me that the completion of the renovations will be part of my healing process. He suggested that my progress is like an "unfinished symphony."

It made so much sense. Even as I write this, I think how profound those words are and how much I need to complete that symphony, with the grace of God, the help of Dr. Gary Read, my psychologist, Dr. Christine Tomcheck, my psychiatrist, and, of course, time.

26th July 2020

This is first time I can remember the 26th of July falling on a Sunday again. That means the early hours of Monday, 27th July will mark exactly five years since the incident occurred.

Same day, same date. It's a haunting thought.

I've been feeling low all day. I've tried to keep busy, but I've felt increasingly anxious and drained. All my emotions came flooding back so strongly, my legs gave way, and I fell to the floor, weeping.

It must be over!

It must be the last time I remember this.

My husband had to help me off the floor and kept watch over me for some time.

27th July 2020

I woke up at 4:38, everything about the incident fresh in my mind.

It must STOP!

I must learn how to deal with this, to cleanse myself emotionally and physically but the thought has become more and more daunting.

3 August 2020

A session with my psychologist revealed this:

Do not continue to live it. As much as I try not to think about it, I suffer from incessant flashbacks and experience constant reminders. I'm sure that most people with P.T.S.D. suffer flashbacks, and at times have set-backs.

Do not become a victim. I still don't know how or where this statement will lead me, but I'm hoping (although I haven't had much hope over the last five years) that it will turn out well, and I will become stronger.

I did it to protect my family. I keep hearing this statement, not only from my doctors but also from family, friends, and strangers. Although I know I did it for exactly that reason, I find it hard to comprehend. My judgement and my religion are conflicted. I battle most with this thought.

I must stop beating myself up about it. As I have been a practicing Christian all my life, and my actions on that night contradicted my beliefs.

It was self-defence. Agreed, but it doesn't make it less painful. It hurts to think about it, and it hurts more to talk about it.

23rd August 2020

Level 2 Lockdown.

During these years of living with P.T.S.D., I've noticed a steady decline in my health, and I've started suffering from severe headaches.

The stress I feel in my shoulders and neck is increasing along with the pain in my arms, but I'm reluctant to take additional medication.

NOTE TO my husband, Rocky, and my daughters, Shante and Tania:

Please remember me the way I was before all this.

oooOooo

During the COVID lockdown, when we were at our holiday home in Hartebeespoort, we met a couple in a peculiar way. As we were forbidden to leave, I had to get my monthly medicinal script emailed to me, and when he went to collect it, my husband had to have it on his person.

It had been raining off and on, and when he returned to the estate, the low-lying entrance to the bridge had flooded. He was stuck in the middle of the bridge, and our neighbours Sarah and Sibu helped tow his car. We have since become good friends, almost a second family.

oooOooo

During the COVID lockdown period, we were invited to the home of friends on the estate, where we casually met several other couples. After initial introductions, we all settled in our chairs.

I was uncomfortable being in the company of so many people, so it had been our intention to meet and greet, then leave. Whilst I was trying to settle my nerves, a guest caught me by surprise, saying, "... it seems you're very skilled with a firearm," and made the shooting gesture with his hand.

I jolted back in my chair and sat still for a few moments, trying to catch my breath. I held back my tears but at the same time my eyes searched desperately for my husband in the group of people. It instantly crossed my mind to find the nearest exit and run. Tightly gripping the arms of the chair, I replied with the first thought that popped into my mind. "I still suffer with P.T.S.D." Fearing the conversation wouldn't end there, I went in search of my husband, afraid to look anyone in the eye.

By the following morning, my mood had become sombre again. I couldn't stop the tears as I asked my husband if I would suffer for the rest of my life whenever someone brought up the subject.

Dear Lord, You know my heart, please let these futile conversations be few and far between.

25 August 2020

I haven't been driving much since the incident. Fortunately, my husband has been able to take me to doctor's appointments when necessary.

But today, I had to try to drive through to the house, and my anxiety was off the charts. I paced around the apartment with the keys in my hand, telling myself I had to find the confidence to get in my car and drive again.

I eventually convinced myself to at least walk to the car. I sat, hands shaking, as I tried and failed several times to put the key in the ignition, I collapsed, sobbing with my head on the steering wheel.

I felt pathetic, inadequate, and a waste of a human being, still breathing air.

I know I need to take baby steps, but it's been so long. When will I be some sort of normal again?

31 August 2020

It seemed my feelings are running parallel to the progress at the house. We needed to upgrade the security before I could even attempt to go back there.

A Comrades athlete has been brutally attacked whilst cycling in the Magaliesburg area, and the news of it made me ill and low. I empathize with him and his loved ones, knowing we can no longer feel safe in this country, where crime seems to lurk around every corner.

My psychologist said that hearing or seeing human tragedy would resurface my trauma, and that I would be sensitive to this kind of information for some time. He said that although it would sometimes be triggered, it was imperative that I avoid another big incident.

I had to refrain from watching any kind of media or TV shows that could be a potential trigger.

1 September 2020

Today, although I felt vulnerable, I managed to drive to the house again. I brought my firearm with me. I opened the door to the study and stood motionless surveying the paperwork that has not been filed for the last five years.

Then it occurred to me that on another level, I was thinking of moving back to the house, perhaps into my eldest daughter's room for the time being. I want to do this so my husband wouldn't have to continue driving up and down each day. He's under enough strain.

I must persevere and try extra hard, no matter how I feel or how difficult it may be. This may be a slow introduction into settling back into the house.

8 September 2020

A massive milestone for me today! I managed to drive from Bedfordview to Hartebeespoort Dam. I haven't driven much since the incident.

I was hyperventilating at the apartment and decided to take additional meds to calm myself, but I drove safely and carefully as I always do.

For most people, driving is an everyday occurrence, but for me, it was a massive achievement. It was a great feeling when I arrived safely at my destination. My daughters, who have always given me tremendous support, were elated on my behalf.

It was a big deal!

25th September 2020

I'm a firm believer that God is the author of my life..... I can only pen what happens to me during or after the fact.

Perhaps what we experienced in our home has been the truest test of my faith.

14 October 2020

On looking back, I realize that I had to be lost in some way to find myself again.

29th November 2020

I cannot say if time has made me understand that what I did was the primal instinct of a mother and wife to protect those I love. I've been told that we're all born with the fight or flight instinct, which rears its ugly head only when we're pushed to the point of no return.

A little note to potential readers: I hope and pray that if perhaps, something I've written strikes a chord, let it remind you that *you are never alone in this.* God bless.

5th December 2020

While I was waiting to see my nephrologist during my bi-annual visit, I noticed and tried to understand why every patient who came in had slumped shoulders, as though they were carrying a boulder of burdens. Although I've noticed this before, it struck home that there is indeed a tragedy behind every mask and it comes in all shapes and sizes.

21 December 2020

I've become afraid to put pen to paper, knowing it will affect my emotional state. Trying to recall the details that come back to me in drips and drabs makes me dejected and disillusioned. I'm exhausted, so very tired of crying. But bear with me, please. I find I can only write when I feel strongest and stop before my emotions get the better of me.

I'm still alone in the apartment, and it has been suggested that I may be self-isolating. Am I? I've only thought about it now that it's been pointed out to me.

I've been meaning to reduce my smoking because of my polycystic kidney disease, which is beginning to show signs of deterioration, as expected. But I'm battling my habit. Quitting means additional stress. I want to get to a place where I'm not constantly fearful and looking over my shoulder.

It is unfortunate that my husband's brother hasn't been to visit his ailing mother for the past few years. Seeing the pressure my husband is under trying to be there for me and my mother-in-law puts me in low spirits. At times, I feel excluded and neglected. If my brother-in-law could relieve us of a little pressure, perhaps my husband and I could heal together. Perhaps we could spend more time together and I could get the attention, love, and care I so desperately crave and need.

Whenever we try to get away for a weekend, my mother-in-law has to come along. Her negativity is detrimental to my emotional state, exacerbating my trauma and delaying my healing. She unfortunately has no filter and can't understand what triggers my P.T.S.D.

Even five years after the incident, certain subjects and words are taboo. I have come to learn that it's the nature of the disorder.

30 December 2020

I've been experiencing many low days, and I'm wondering whether it's because we haven't moved back to our house yet. I want and so desperately need to reach the next step in my healing. I need something tangible to measure my progress. It's always on my mind that I'm clawing at life.

Early January 2021

Our domestic, had just tested positive for COVID, yet another delay in moving back to our house. My polycystic kidney disease places me at high risk for contracting COVID, so I have to avoid being in the same environment as someone who has it.

8th January 2021

For a few days now I've been going to the house daily to unpack and repack as much as I can. I've geared myself up to stay at the house until night descends, trying to see how far I can push myself and remain in the place where it all happened.

I'd been doing well, or so I thought, until I collapsed on our bedroom floor and broke down completely. I wondered if I was wasting my time and energy trying to make a go at moving back, and with that came doubts about the strength of our marriage.

I sat on the floor, weak and incoherent, weeping non-stop when I remembered that sombre night and the intruder lying on his back on the floor. Will this ever go away? Will I have to relive this forever?

22nd January 2021

It's been a tough day at the house again and I took additional medication to calm myself, but I also know I don't want to become dependent on it.

I was reluctant to call my husband to take me back to the apartment, since I'd only been at the house for an hour. I thought he might get angry if I interrupted his work day again. I never want to be a burden. The anguish is exponential.

I didn't ask to be in this situation — it was thrust upon me. All day, I couldn't shake my feelings.

My sleeping pattern has been drastically impacted once more. My psychiatrist prescribed additional medication to take at night, in addition to my regular anxiety meds and sleeping tablet.

23rd January 2021

For the first time since the incident, I woke up feeling as though I'd gotten much needed rest. I know the additional meds are only a temporary solution. I still I have much work to do on myself.

3rd February 2021

The pressure, anxiety, and stress levels are ever increasing.

Now in addition to our domestic, my mother-in-law is suffering with COVID. We're trying to support them both while avoiding being infected ourselves.

I've failed to drive several times, firstly due to my fear of driving and secondly, being approached by someone at an intersection. Fear and anxiety now hold me in their clutches, squeezing every breath out of me, a little each day.

Somehow, and I cannot explain why, I don't feel grounded. Could it be that we're still living in the apartment where *temporary* has become six years. In some ways, living here has aided my healing process, but I wonder if I need to move on.

My sleep is still erratic and filled with nightmares. My days are endless memories of the incident, which still cause pain in both my arms and chest. My psychiatrist has added more medication to reduce the flashbacks and help level my sleep patterns. She's concerned that going back to the house will reactivate the trauma, and I'll slip off the path to recovery. She explained that my incident could be likened to that of a war veteran going back into the war zone. She reiterated that I need to be in a safe environment.

The professionals in my life are constantly reminding me not to feel guilty or blame myself. Even whilst writing this, I still go back to the reason for my guilt. *I did commit a grave sin.*

I have realized that suffering with P.T.S.D. has placed insurmountable stress on my marriage, and in turn, my stress levels keep skyrocketing. It seems to have snowballed.

6th February 2021

Whilst living in this world that P.T.S.D. has created, I've come to realize it has had a massive impact on those who love me.

It's difficult to internalize information at a regular pace. It takes time, and when people push for immediate answers, it feels as though I am being cornered.

Even loved ones, who spend most of their time around me, still don't fully understand the impact their words or the environments have on me. I try to understand their position, but they've never been through it themselves. It's not tangible, but it's there.

I talked with husband about the sessions with my psychiatrist. His response left me in shock. He said he'd forgotten about the invasion, and that I was the only constant reminder. I was dumbfounded and so hurt, I didn't know what to do with myself. My self-blame became overwhelming. I felt as though my whole life and heart had fallen away.

I became even more lost and dejected, I was hurt and I had no idea where to go.

11th February 2021

Over time, I have come to realize how easily people use words such as "kill" or "die." Could it be because they've never experienced a real life death balance before?

16th February 2021

Things that I used to enjoy doing, such as cooking, photography or drawing, are no longer a part of me. My imagination has become increasingly crippled.

29th March 2021

Today I was back at the house and found myself frozen in the bedroom looking out the sliding door where the intruders had entered.

I was unable to step onto the balcony as it would mean I'd be retracing my steps of that night where the second intruder lost his life.

April 2021

I blindly exposed myself by staying over at the house from Sunday to Monday. There's no handbook to tell me how to face my fear. I'm just a simple woman pushing her boundaries.

When I shared this with my psychologist, he was over the moon to hear that we'd managed to sleep there, if only for one night. I'd decided to sleep on my husband's side of the bed, so I'd avoid the position I was in on the night of the incident, and I wouldn't see the door where they forced entry.

Even though doing this was a difficult, I think I ought to congratulate myself for taking that step. I hold onto my psychologist's words: "I must walk with the strength I've got."

May 2021

I've driven to the house for several successive days, but I've needed to take an additional calming tablet. I feel fatigued, and the intense headaches have returned. The unrelenting anxiety is overwhelming.

I have to deal with all this on my own. My husband is working in Cape Town from Monday to Friday, and I'm feeling quite helpless, disillusion always waiting around the corner.

20th May 2021

It's been several years since the invasion, and I've only just asked myself this very pertinent question:

"If I cannot forgive myself, how do I move on?"

Friday, 21st May to Monday, 24th May 2021

I have decided to take a bold step and sleep at the house all weekend.

31st May 2021

Dr. Read told me not to give up, to keep trying. I need to consider this a transit lounge and keep moving slowly.

Most people would think I'm nuts for trying to go back to the place where it began, but I want to empower myself rather than feeling overcome by the invaders. If I leave our home, I want it to be on my terms, not theirs!

June 2021

How sad life has become when a mother's champion is her daughter! The very same daughter she protected during the invasion.

At times, I still ask myself what the point is of having survived?

14th June 2021

Another year has gone by, and the date of the incident is again slowly creeping closer. I'm awfully stressed and emotional. I don't want to feel these emotions year after year.

15th June 2021

My question to myself today: "Am I the victim or the victor?"

10th July 2021

Life is such a rat race. No-one looks left or right to acknowledge the person next to them. How will they ever notice someone in such deep, dark unrelenting pain?

18th July 2021

I've made the decision that my short-term goal now is to leave the apartment and move back into our home. Living in the apartment has been extremely helpful with my healing process, but it's time to move on.

We've decided that this would be the time to try to live there whilst finishing off the refurbishments. We know the challenges and I'm prepared to give it everything I have.

20th July 2021

About a month ago. I agreed that one of my sisters should stay with us while she's in the process of selling her old house.

Today, knowing that I'm moving back into our house, I feel afraid. I haven't been sleeping well for some time. I'm petrified, especially since my husband is working in Cape Town again. I don't have the safety net I need.

I'm constantly tearful and have taken additional calming meds. I'm very aware that I have to live and sleep with my firearm by my side, yet next to it lies my Bible — a complete paradox, straight out of a psychological thriller.

And I pray, "*Lord, please guide me.*"

21st July 2021

I've noticed that in conversations between my husband and I regarding the incident we've been through, I immediately block it out without revealing the turmoil within me.

For others, each day is a chosen path for their tomorrow, which is as it should be. Whereas for me, life resembles a waterfall that suddenly stopped in midstream and hasn't moved forward for years.

I'm moving back to the house as I consider it part of my healing process. I need to find out if I can do this before I can permanently close the door to that chapter.

This is my chapter, and I have to face it alone. I'm afraid, but I'll push forward, one moment at a time.

23rd July 2021

My life has become a complete contradiction. I sleep with my Bible on one side of me and my firearm on the other, fully aware that this is not *living*. I question now whether it's even surviving.

Flashbacks consume my dreams, and I wake me up in a cold sweat. *I felt pressure on my chest, and a firearm was shoved into my mouth as I screamed my husband's name...............*

When I awoke it took me some time to realize it was a dream only. My throat was painfully sore and dry from screaming. I spent the rest of the night awake, holding my firearm, walking around the house, waiting, watching. And sleep eluded me once again.

27th July 2021

It's the sixth year since the invasion. I don't know how to explain to those I love that being back at the house for this short period has made me want to escape.

I'm making every effort to retake my home, the good feelings and experiences. But I feel a sense of chaos. I find no comfort, and there are moments when I feel I don't belong. The weeping does not subside.

And then, sometimes I think I may be expecting too much of myself.

28th July 2021

To those who suffer with P.T.S.D.:

There are no hard and fast rules for going through trauma. It's a personal journey you take alone, just you and your raw, unfiltered, unadulterated feelings and emotions.

Know that the time it takes to recover is yours and yours alone.

2nd August 2021

As I arrived back at the apartment this afternoon, I felt the stress lift from my shoulders. After speaking to my psychologist this morning, I decided to go to the house during the day only and spend my nights at the apartment.

I'm relieved, not only because I won't have to spend an uncomfortable night alone in the bedroom, but also because I don't want my sister to see me in this state. I don't want her to deal with or witness my P.T.S.D.

I didn't realize how stressed I've been for the last few days until I got back to the apartment. I was so drained, so tired.

4th August 2021

Every day, I drive to the house to check on the renovation and unpack as much as I can manage. Today, I was holding the steering wheel tightly, praying for God to keep me safe. At some point, I changed my mind and decided to drive straight to the police station to renew my firearm license. I prayed silently again before I left the car, praying for strength and guidance at this hellhole of a police station I never wanted to see again. I was afraid. Alone and afraid.

Later, I decided not to go to the house, took my additional meds and drove back to the apartment. I thanked God from the bottom of my heart and soul that He's with me during these brave and untimely decisions. I felt a silly sense of achievement. I'd come through yet another storm in my P.T.S.D. journey. It would never have been possible without God by my side.

My instincts tell me not to give up.

5th August 2021

Being at our house, surrounded by its architectural beauty is indescribably serene and wonderful. Yet every sound — a car door closing, a garage door opening, the barking of a dog, the voices of neighbours, even the gentle rustling of leaves — makes me realize I have to re-adapt.

My stress level becomes elevated, until realization sets in, and I stop hearing every sound as a threat.

I still constantly mull over the incident, and I know I broke one of the ten-commandments. It has hit me hard, and I'm very aware that I'll carry this burden to the end of my days.

1 September 2021

P.T.S.D. is insanely visceral, and it hasn't helped that everyone in the country is wearing masks to avoid COVID.

My family has been tremendously understanding, avoiding wearing dark masks in my presence, especially black ones. I find that although these are the people I love and risked my life for, I can't t look them in the eye when they wear dark or black masks.

Driving through a small village near Cape Town, where hordes of people are in one area, gave me angst. I realized it would be mundane for most people, but it was exacerbated by my trauma.

At the time, I didn't think about it, but my body and mind immediately looked for an escape route, I've been told that this is a routine to be expected by those suffering from P.T.S.D.

I've been in Cape Town now for three weeks, and I don't quite know how to describe it, but it's almost as though one layer of my mask has been removed. And it feels so good.

3rd September 2021

I did a little introspection this morning. I'm thinking back to that pivotal moment in our lives and the ages my daughters were at the time.

Our eldest had just turned 29. Our grandson was one month and two days old. Our youngest hadn't turned 19 yet and was taking a gap year between matriculating and studying.

And there we were in that moment when our lives were ripped apart. Today, the hairs on the back of my neck still rise when I think about it. My back immediately straightens, perhaps in a defending mode, I don't know. I don't like feeling this way at all, but apparently this is my new normal.

We're here right now, alive and breathing.

This is a revelation for me, an epiphany.

5th November 2021

I've taken a bold stand in my mind and decided that I can't let the intruders write the story of my life!

7th November 2021

It's a time of agony. I yearn to go to bed peacefully without waiting for the next attack.

12th November 2021

I often wonder why people use terminology such as "you killed it," when they could simply say "job well done" or "you exceeded my expectations" or "brilliant job." That and similar expressions triggers my trauma and I immediately want to protect those I love.

There are times when I dislike myself, when I see people who have been injured in wars and feel I should be more grateful that this incident left me without physical disabilities or worse. I don't like who I am or how I feel. But it does beg the question of survivor's guilt.

10th January 2022

Today I googled the word "pilates," thinking that it might assist my healing. The first article that popped up was a photo of warrior women with the heading "girlfriend, robbers." The year 2015 stood out. A video clip of a woman who deterred a robbery in her home came up. My mind was reeling and my body went into shock yet again.

As a rule, I avoid anything of this sort. I'm still not ready to deal with the emotional turmoil it evokes, I'm not strong enough to deal with anything remotely similar to our invasion.

I'm seriously doubting my decision to move back into our house. In my heart of hearts, I want to make the decision to stay or go based solely on my own terms, not those of the invaders.

February 2022

I sometimes think my mind has been my weakness, but that's wrong, it's been my pillar of strength.

Countless times whilst sitting at my laptop to write, I've thought I would rather be writing a fantasy novel than this crude introspection.

When my husband works away from home, I feel he's at times divorced from my emotions and constant triggers.

There have been times where I've felt the need to end all of this, and would look over at my firearm.

Each morning when I look in the mirror, I see more fine lines on my face and the image staring back at me is repugnant. This is not the person I used to be, yet we all know that the mirror tells no lies.

15 February 2022

It's sad in a way that the independence of driving my car has been snatched from me. I'm unable to take a taxi or car service for fear the driver may be wearing a black mask or just remind me of the assailants, though my thoughts and fears are no fault of theirs.

17*th* February 2022

As I sit alone in the apartment, everyone around me continues their daily lives. I think about the bold step I've been anticipating. My husband will be in Cape Town, so I'll go back to the house where it all happened alone nearly seven years later.

I pray that our good Lord will be by my side.

23*rd* February 2022

It is now the fourth night I've slept alone at the house. Each morning, my daughters and husband call to ask how my night has been. For three of those nights, I've taken additional calming meds as well as my regular P.T.S.D. medication I constantly get out of bed double, triple checking that doors and windows are secure until I'm eventually so tired that the meds take over. However, last night, I tried going to sleep without the additional meds and was awake at 4am, the incident playing over and over in my mind. The incident occurred just after 4am on that fateful day.

For past few weeks, I've noticed bruises on my body again, meaning I've been injuring myself during my sleep.

28*th* February 2022

My psychologist is deeply concerned that being back in the house may gradually break me down. I need to give thought to what would be best for me. I have to re-learn how to empower myself, to be patient and forgive my imperfections.

31*st* March 2022

As time goes by, I look at things anew, almost like a child who sees something exciting for the first time.

I see things differently, but it's always through the haze of P.T.S.D.

19 April 2022

An odd thing I've noticed in the society we live in, is that people's feelings are so often negated.

25th June 2022

Almost seven years ago, God gave me famine. I pray that from this day forward, He will bless me with seven more years of life. Hopefully, this time, it will be a life of harvest.

8th August 2022

If this has happened to you on some level, take a bold step and remember *never* let it define you!

Word of Thanks

It's only by the grace of God that we are here to share our story.

Thank you to my dearest family who are still supporting me through this journey — Rocky, Shante and Tania. I don't have enough adjectives in my vocabulary to describe how much I love you all. I cannot describe in words how blessed I am with the help and understanding each of you has given me, both together and individually.

You are the elixir of my life.

Thank you to my amazing doctors who have walked this cobble-stone journey with me. I can honestly say that I do not know where I would have been on this journey had it not been for the both of you holding my hand along the way.

Psychologist, Dr. Gary Read, *MA(Psych) MA9 Clin Psych) JUDE (Rhodes) PhD. (Pret)*

Psychiatrist, Dr. Christine Tomcheck, *BSc (UCT), MBChB (UCT), FCPsych(SA).*

Thank you for still continuing to help me through these rough and testy waters.

Thank you to our friends and extended family, most especially for being the strength and support for our loving daugthers — Leo, Bruno, and my little champ. (Nana loves you, sweetheart.)

To my husband, with love

In the first year of all this turmoil in our lives, I saw you every day, but I missed you.

We were both hurting. I shared nothing. But I listened. I heard you. I wonder now, did you ever hear me?

Edna da Rocha

Acknowledgements

Family Rocky, my husband
   Shante, our youngest daughter
   Tania, our eldest daughter
   Leo, our son-in-law
   Linda, my sister
   Friends Gavin De Agrella, security and friend
   Sarah and Sibu, dearest friends
   Practitioner Dr Struwig (GP)
   Psychiatrist Dr. Tomcheck
   Psychololgist Dr. Read
   Special thanks and acknowledgement to the authors for their inspirational poems.
   Cover photography by Author, Edna da Rocha

I alone cannot change the world,
but I can cast a stone
across the water
to create many ripples
Mother Theresa

What I have come to realize is that when you suffer from P.T.S.D, there really is no time-line. You will feel isolated and alone, as your experience and emotions will be yours only.

When I felt I had nothing, I tried often to put my thoughts on paper knowing that God will always be my rock.

I have learnt that there is something more frightening that your own death, and that is the fear of losing someone you love.

Some humble advice, if I may – try, fail, pick yourself up and try again.

Mental Health Resource List

South African Federation for Mental Health (SAFMH)
This organization will put you in touch with the appropriate mental health resources you may require.
Contact details:
Website: www.safmh.org[1]
Email: info@samfh.org
Tel: (+27)(0) 11 781-1852

People Opposed to Woman Abuse (POWA)
POWA provides counselling both over the phone and in person.
Contact details:
Website: http:/www.powa.co.za
Tel: (011) 642-4345
Email: info@powa.co.za
Social Media: Facebook and Twitter

---

1. http://www.safmh.org